TRAVEL WITH THE GREAT EXPLORERS

Explore with
Jacques Cartier

Marie Powell

Crabtree Publishing Company
www.crabtreebooks.com

Crabtree Publishing Company
www.crabtreebooks.com

Author: Marie Powell
Publishing plan research
   and development: Reagan Miller
Managing editor: Tim Cooke
Editors: Kathy Middleton, Shannon Welbourn
Designer: Lynne Lennon
Picture manager: Sophie Mortimer
Design manager: Keith Davis
Editorial director: Lindsey Lowe
Children's publisher: Anne O'Daly
Production coordinator
   and prepress technician: Tammy McGarr
Print coordinator: Katherine Berti

Produced by Brown Bear Books for
Crabtree Publishing Company

Photographs:
Front Cover: John Gould: tr; istockphoto: cr; Shutterstock: Marcel
Clemens br; Topfoto: The Granger Collection main.

Interior: Bridgeman Art Library: 11t; Dreamstime: 22b;
Getty Images: Archive Photos 5t; istockphoto: 6-7t;
Library of Congress: 11b, 12t, 14t, 19r, 27t, 29;
Public Domain: Base Joconde 10; Robert Hunt Library: 28-29b;
Shutterstock: 4t, 6l, 17c, 17b, 21r, 21bl, 22t, 26, Antonio Abrignani 23b,
Barbara Barbour 24, Jeni Foto 28t, Olga Labusova 27b,
Denis Radovanovic 25r, SF Foto 20, Elena Yakusheva 23t;
Thinkstock: Dorling Kindersley RF 13t, istockphoto 5b, 6r, 12bl, 13b,
14b, 15t, 16, 25b, Photos.com 17t, 18; Topfoto: Artmedia/HIP 19t.

All other artwork and maps © Brown Bear Books Ltd.

Library and Archives Canada Cataloguing in Publication

Powell, Marie, author
      Explore with Jacques Cartier / Marie Powell.

(Travel with the great explorers)
Includes index.
Issued in print and electronic formats.
ISBN 978-0-7787-1426-2 (bound).--ISBN 978-0-7787-1432-3 (pbk.).--
ISBN 978-1-4271-7583-0 (pdf).--ISBN 978-1-4271-7577-9 (html)

      1. Cartier, Jacques, 1491-1557--Juvenile literature. 2. Explorers--
France--Biography--Juvenile literature. 3. Explorers--Canada--
Biography--Juvenile literature. 4. Canada--Discovery and
exploration--French--Juvenile literature. 5. Saint Lawrence River--
Discovery and exploration--Juvenile literature. 6. Canada--History--
To 1663 (New France)--Juvenile literature. I. Title.

FC301.C37P68 2014   j971.01'13092   C2014-903657-4
                                               C2014-903658-2

Library of Congress Cataloging-in-Publication Data

CIP available at the Library of Congress

Crabtree Publishing Company

www.crabtreebooks.com   1-800-387-7650

Printed in Hong Kong/082014/BK20140613

Published in Canada
Crabtree Publishing
616 Welland Ave.
St. Catharines, ON
L2M 5V6

Published in the United States
Crabtree Publishing
PMB 59051
350 Fifth Avenue, 59th Floor
New York, New York 10118

Published in the United Kingdom
Crabtree Publishing
Maritime House
Basin Road North, Hove
BN41 1WR

Published in Australia
Crabtree Publishing
3 Charles Street
Coburg North
VIC, 3058

CONTENTS

Meet the Boss

Jacques Cartier was a French explorer who made three voyages to North America. He explored the west coast of Newfoundland and along the St. Lawrence River, opening Canada to French settlement.

MYSTERY BACKGROUND

+ Did explorer study navigation?

Jacques Cartier was born in 1491, in the French fishing port of St. Malo. We don't know much about his early life. His family likely made its living by fishing. He may have learned **navigation** at a naval school. He married Mary Catherine des Granches in 1520, and they settled in St. Malo.

TRAVEL UPDATE

French fishers head abroad

★ Some people think Cartier may have sailed across the Atlantic as a young man. After explorer John Cabot discovered Newfoundland (when Cartier was only six years old), St. Malo fishermen sailed there for the good cod fishing off the Grand Banks. Cartier likely started as a sailor on these fishing trips.

COD!

There were so many cod on the Grand Banks off Newfoundland it was said that fishermen could drop buckets into the ocean and pull them up full of fish.

PERSONAL AMBITION

★ **Explorer out for himself**

★ **Hard streak in his character**

By the time he was about 42 years old, Cartier was both a ship's captain and a master **pilot** guiding ships into ports. Some people think ambition drove him to search for the legendary **Northwest Passage**—a sea route to Asia across the top of North America. He may have wanted to impress the King of France. He was so determined, he was even prepared to mistreat the native peoples to be the first to find the route.

Did you know?

Cartier's wife later became godmother to a native Brazilian girl brought to St. Malo by a trading expedition.

BRAZIL NUT!

☞ **How does explorer know Portuguese?**

Because Cartier could speak Portugese, many people believed he must have sailed to Brazil, a colony of Portugal, and learned to speak it there. His visit to Brazil as a young sailor was confirmed in his journals.

Where Are We Heading?

Cartier's travels took him deep into what is now Canada, but he had actually been looking for China. The Northwest Passage was thought to be a shortcut for voyages from Europe to Asia.

OFF TO CHINA

- Mysterious empire has rich goods
- Make big profits in the luxury trade

China was a potential trading partner for Europe but little was known about the country. In the 1400s, countries like France relied on trade with countries in Asia for valuable goods such as gold, silk, and spices such as cloves. Spices were prized for flavor and for curing disease. China was valued for silk, porcelain, and tea, among other goods. These items were expensive, partly because merchants had to carry the goods over land through other countries.

 Weather Forecast

SHORTCUT FROZEN OVER

The main purpose of Cartier's first voyage was to find a sea route to Asia around the top of North America. This was known as the Northwest Passage. It was not found until the early 20th century. Although the route existed, the sea was frozen for much of the year, so it was not very useful.

TRAVEL UPDATE

Explorer sailed inland

★ On Cartier's second voyage, two Iroquois prisoners helped him navigate the Hochelaga River, now known as the St. Lawrence River. Cartier and his men traveled up the St. Lawrence about 500 miles (800 km) to the Iroquois village of Stadacona, and from there to a settlement called Hochelaga—today part of Montreal.

BLOCKED

Cartier hoped the St. Lawrence would lead him into the heart of North America. In fact, the river was blocked by rapids that prevented ships from sailing up it.

TELL ME A STORY

★ Mystery kingdom full of promise...

★ ...but does it really exist?

Local native peoples told Cartier about a kingdom called Saguenay, with lots of gold and other **resources**. On his third voyage, Cartier set out to find Saguenay. He looked for it without success until winter's arrival forced him to stop. Perhaps Saguenay did not exist. It may be that native peoples told him the stories to encourage him to move inland—and to leave them alone.

My Explorer Journal

★ Imagine you were an Iroquois trying to convince Cartier that a rich kingdom like Saguenay really existed. What kind of details would you use to persuade him to go try to find it?

Jacques Cartier's Travels in Canada

Jacques Cartier sailed into the Gulf of St. Lawrence to try to find a route to Asia. Instead he found a river that led to the heart of what is now Canada. He returned twice more, following much the same route each time.

CANADA

Hochelaga
This Iroquois village stood near what is now Montreal. Cartier built a double fort nearby that he called Fort Charlesbourg Royal. The French occupied the fort for a few years before abandoning it.

GREAT LAKES

Lachine Rapids
From the heights of Mont Royal (Montreal), Cartier could see rapids blocking his passage upstream. He realized that the St. Lawrence was not his hoped-for water route to Asia—the Northwest Passage.

NORTH AMERICA

Gaspé Peninsula
Cartier set up a cross at the mouth of Gaspé Bay and claimed the land for France in 1534. Chief Donnacona objected, saying it belonged to the Iroquois. When Cartier departed, he took Donnacona's two sons with him. Whether they left willingly is uncertain.

Stadacona

This Iroquois village near what is now Quebec City was home to Chief Donnacona and his family. Cartier built Fort Stadacona nearby.

Gulf of St. Lawrence

Cartier showed his great skill as a navigator in his exploration of the vast Gulf of St. Lawrence. He explored numerous inlets and bays as he sought a route into the North American continent.

North Atlantic Ocean

Isle des Oiseaux

Cartier called this tiny island off Newfoundland Isle des Oiseaux—the Island of Birds. Now called Funk Island, Cartier's crew shot many sea birds there for food. It was also where they saw their first polar bear.

Newfoundland

North Atlantic Ocean

Key

• • • • • ▶ First journey

- - - ▶ Second and third journeys

Locator map

Meet the Crew

Did you know?

Spain had been building an empire in the Caribbean and South America since 1492. Other European rulers funded exploration to try to copy Spain.

Jacques Cartier was ambitious and selfish. But he owed much of his success to many people he either knew personally or was connected with.

LONG LIVE THE KING!

+ French monarch eager for new lands

King Francis I ruled France from 1515 until his death in 1547. Francis had already funded an exploration by Giovanni da Verrazzano along the east coast of the **New World**. In 1533, the king asked Cartier to search for new lands. That led to Cartier's first voyage in 1534. The king also supported Cartier in two more voyages to Canada. He later sent Jean Francois de la Rocque, Sieur de Roberval to found a settlement and spread "the Holy Catholic Faith."

ITALIAN PIONEER

☛ Verrazzano reaches America

☛ Tragically killed in Caribbean

Giovanni da Verrazzano was an Italian explorer who sailed across the Atlantic Ocean in 1524 on behalf of King Francis I of France. Some people think Cartier may have sailed with him. In 1528, Verrazzano was killed in the Caribbean, so the king turned to Cartier to continue exploring on his behalf.

COMPETITORS

+ Roberval lags behind

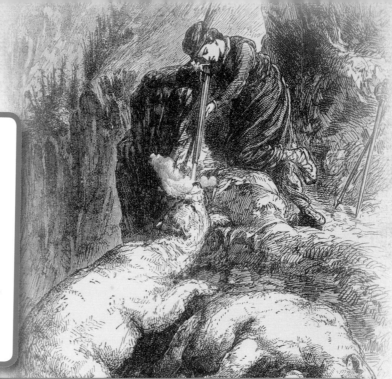

Jean Francois de la Rocque, Sieur de Roberval was a nobleman with close ties to the king's court. He led an expedition to Canada in 1541. King Francis I made him the commander of Cartier's third voyage to found a **colony** for France. Delayed by storms, Roberval was late reaching Canada. Cartier had already built and abandoned two forts, and was on his way back to France.

VICTIM OF LOVE

☞ Noblewoman abandoned

☞ Left to die on island

Marguerite de La Rocque de Roberval was a relative who sailed with Roberval to Canada. She fell in love with a young man on the journey. Disapproving, Roberval left her with her lover and a servant on an island in the Gulf of St. Lawrence. Only Marguerite survived. She was rescued by fishermen some years later. She had hunted animals for food and lived in a cave.

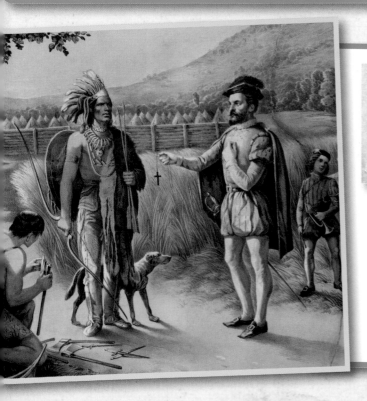

STORYTELLER

★ Chief Donnacona helps explorer

★ Stories have audiences spellbound

Chief Donnacona from the Stadacona Iroquois met Cartier on his first voyage to Canada. On his second voyage, the chief traveled with Cartier back to France. He turned out to be a great storyteller and told the French stories about the kingdom of Saguenay, which he said had supplies of gold, rubies, and other valuable goods.

Check Out the Ride

Jacques Cartier lived at a time when Europeans were building better ships. This technological advance helped Europeans travel more widely and spread their influence around the world.

TAKE AN OAR!

- Longboats used near the coast
- Slower than native vessels

Longboats were large, open rowboats used for exploring coasts and bays. The longboat could carry several men. It was powered by a sail and by men rowing with oars. Cartier and his crew used longboats to explore rivers. They were surprised at how easily canoes paddled by the native peoples could overtake their boats.

Dig it out!

The Mi'kmaq and other native peoples used canoes. They were made by hollowing out logs or covering the frame of a hull with sheets of bark from birch trees.

MASTER SEAMAN

+ Cartier sails many ships

On his first voyage in 1534, Cartier had two ships, with two or three masts and square sails. The boats were large, in case Cartier wanted to carry quantities of goods to trade. He was a master pilot, and his crew of 60 men benefited. They crossed the Atlantic in only 20 days and lost no men on the voyage. On his second voyage in 1535, Cartier took a crew of 110 and three ships. Although separated by storms, the ships met again near Newfoundland.

TRAVEL UPDATE

Cutting-edge technology

★ In the 15th and 16th centuries, European countries used ocean-going ships called "carracks." These had three or four masts, with square sales on the front two masts and a triangular lateen sail at the back that could catch wind blowing from any direction. The ship was big enough to carry a large crew and provisions, as well as cargo to bring home, making it a favorite with trading merchants.

Did you know?

There were no horses in the Americas before Europeans arrived. In fact, it was the Spaniards who first introduced horses to the New World.

TWO BY TWO...

★ **It's a ship, not an ark!**

★ **Animals everywhere**

On his third voyage, In May 1541, Cartier had five ships, carrying cattle, goats, hogs, and other animals. He intended to breed the animals so the colonists could begin to raise livestock. Soon after he arrived in Canada, Cartier sent two ships back to France. They carried messages for the king. They may have asked the king to send more men.

Solve It with Science

Cartier was a master seaman and had a reputation as an outstanding **cartographer**. He drew maps using the best European technology of the 16th century.

WRITE AWAY!

☞ **Knowledge spreads**

☞ **Explorers rely on old records**

Cartier may have had access to a map based on the 1524 voyage of Giovanni da Verrazzano. He may also have had handwritten notes of landmarks, tides, rocks, hazards and harbors. Cartier would have used a **compass** to indicate the direction of north. It helped sailors figure out which way to go..

MASTER MAPMAKER

★ **Cartier tops the charts**

Cartier was known as a fine navigator and mapmaker. On his first voyage, he created maps and charts as he explored, and wrote many notes that helped him on the return journeys. The map he made of the St. Lawrence River helped guide other explorers. It was the basis of a famous map later drawn by the French explorer Samuel de Champlain who followed Cartier in the early 17th century.

IT'S IN THE STARS

+ Navigating by the stars

By using an **astrolabe**, sailors could measure the height of stars (or the sun) above the horizon. This allowed them to figure out their **latitude**, or position north or south of the equator. At night, sailors could also study the position of **constellations** to see how much they seemed to move after a day's sailing.

WHERE ARE WE?

☞ Cross-staff shows latitude

Cartier probably used a cross-staff. He lined up a cross piece on the staff with the horizon and the **pole star**. By knowing the height of the pole star, he could figure out his latitude, or how far north or south he was.

TRAVEL UPDATE

Where are we now?

★ If sailors could not see the stars to navigate, they used dead reckoning. They determined the ship's speed and direction and used these measurements to calculate their current position and roughly how far they had come from a starting point.

Speedy!

Sailors measured their speed by tying a rope to a log they threw into the sea. They tied knots in the rope and counted how many knots were pulled out after a certain amount of time.

Hanging at Home

Cartier found the winters in Canada to be bitingly cold. It was difficult to keep warm, but the Europeans learned from native peoples how to preserve food and cure diseases.

Did you know?

The average temperature, in the part of Canada where Cartier spent the winter of 1535–1536, dropped as low as 9°F (–13°C). According to Cartier, the snow was as high as the decks of the French ships.

 Weather Forecast

BRRR...IT'S COLD

From November 1535 to April 1536, Cartier and his men were trapped in deep snow. The rivers froze, drinking water froze, and bitter winds blew. Their food ran out, and the crew got sick. Cartier lost so many men, he had to abandon one of his ships.

FIRST FORTRESS

★ **An uncomfortable winter**

★ **One-star accommodation**

Cartier and his men spent the winter on his second voyage at a fort outside the village of the Iroquois chief Donnacona at Stadacona. It is now the site of Quebec City. The fort was very simple. The Frenchmen lived in wooden huts surrounded by a **palisade**, or wall of vertical logs, for protection.

ANOTHER STRONGHOLD

- ☛ Log fort home to colonists
- ☛ Grow your own veggies!

On his third voyage, Cartier built the settlement Charlesbourg Royal. There were two forts with vegetable gardens. Cartier anchored his ships at the lower fort and built about 130 feet (40 m) up the bank for a better defensive position. About 400 colonists spent the winter of 1541 there. After Cartier returned to France, Roberval arrived and spent the next winter there before abandoning the fort in 1543.

> " Our captain had the fort strengthened with large and deep ditches, with a drawbridge, and more timbers."
>
> *Cartier describes taking precautions against attack*

WHAT'S FOR DINNER?

+ Salt with everything

+ What about their blood pressure?

The Iroquois did not use salt, but Cartier and his men preferred their food with salt. As in Europe, the explorers prepared for winter by hunting and fishing, and then salting their food to preserve it. To preserve fish, they would remove the fish heads and stomachs, wash the flesh, salt it, and lay it on rocks or fir branches to dry. They packed food in casks of wet brine (salted water) in a ship's hold to **cure** it.

Meeting and Greeting

The French claimed Canada and named it New France. But it was far from empty. Many native peoples had lived there for centuries. Some welcomed the Europeans—others were more suspicious.

OFF TO A BAD START

☞ **Cartier strikes wrong note**

☞ **Mi'kmaq left unhappy…and cold!**

In 1534, Cartier became the first European to trade with native peoples when he met the Mi'kmaq. In exchange for furs, he swapped knives, **hatchets**, glass beads, and a red cap. He even took the furs they were wearing.

WHAT'S IN A NAME?

★ **Canada gets its name**

★ **Named in error**

King Francis I sent Cartier on a second voyage to continue exploring the New World. Donnacona's sons described where they lived using their word for village—*Kanata*. Cartier misunderstood and named the whole country Canada.

MEETING THE IROQUOIS

+ Cartier gets it wrong (again)...

At the Gaspé Bay, Cartier met the St. Lawrence Iroquois. Chief Donnacona was leading a fishing party. The Iroquois were friendly until Cartier erected a large cross at Percé Rock. He wanted to claim the land for France and for the Christian Church. Donnacona insisted that the land belonged to the Iroquois.

My Explorer Journal

★ It is likely Cartier kidnapped Donnacona's sons—and more Iroquois on a later voyage—and took them to France against their will. Use details in the text to write a letter from Cartier explaining why you did that.

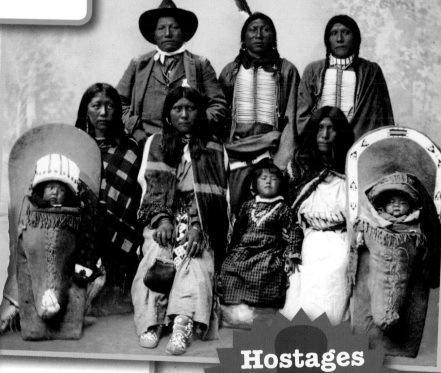

YOU'RE COMING WITH US

☛ Explorer resorts to kidnap

Donnacona had two sons, named Domagaya and Taignoagny. Cartier invited Donnacona and his family onboard his ship—but the invitation was likely a trick. It is believed he **kidnapped** the chief's two sons and took them back to France as proof of his discovery.

Hostages

On his second trip, Cartier kidnapped more Iroquois, including Donnacona. The descendants of the Iroquois still live in North America today.

Return to New France

A year after returning to Europe, Cartier returned to the New World—now called New France. On this second voyage, he behaved even more brutally toward the native peoples than before.

WELCOME HOME!

+ Sons return after a year away

A year after taking Donnacona's sons back with him to Europe, Cartier came back to New France with Domagaya and Taignoagny. They guided him to their village, Stadacona. The St. Lawrence Iroquois held a feast to celebrate the safe return of the chief's sons. But the Iroquois seemed reluctant to let Cartier explore further upriver. Cartier decided that must mean there were valuable resources to be found there.

MMM...CORN

➤ **Explorer visits Iroquois**

➤ **Enjoys a feast**

On his second voyage, Cartier and his men reached Hochelaga. The Iroquois lived in groups in large wooden longhouses. They welcomed Cartier with a feast. They grew corn and made cornbread for their European guests.

SERIAL OFFENDER

★ **Cartier kidnaps more Iroquois**

★ **Only one survives**

When Cartier sailed home from his second voyage, in 1536, he kidnapped a dozen Iroquois, including Donnacona and his sons. All but one died in France. When Cartier returned to Canada again, he told the other Iroquois that their fellows had become powerful lords in France.

Did you know?

After Cartier took Donnacona to France, the Iroquois were led by a new chief named Agona. He was friendly at first, but Agona soon came to distrust Cartier.

TRAVEL UPDATE

What's on the Menu?

★ On visits to Donnacona's village, Cartier saw many vegetables that were new to Europeans—corn, melons, cucumbers, and pumpkins. He was also given the leaves of another **cultivated** plant to smoke—tobacco.

THINGS GO SOUR

☞ **French under attack**

Cartier made his third voyage to New France in 1541. Relations with the Iroquois turned bad when he admitted that Donnacona had died in France. Cartier moved to Charlesbourg Royal for safety. The fort came under constant attack. After the Iroquois killed 35 settlers, Cartier abandoned it and returned to France.

I Love Nature

In New France, Cartier and his men came across all kinds of plants and animals that no European had seen before. Some are still very familiar to us today.

A SWIMMING COW!

+ Looks lovely...tastes nice, too

Cartier and his crew first saw polar bears on Isle des Oiseaux, Newfoundland. In his journal, he described a bear "as big as a cow and white as a swan." The first bear sighted was swimming. The men got into their boats, killed it, and ate it, noting that the meat was "as good to eat as that of a two-year-old heifer (cow)."

NATURE'S BOUNTY

★ **Explorer records trees and plants**

★ **Recognizes some species, not others**

Cartier noted details of many plants and animals in his journals. On his first voyage, he noted such trees as oak, elm, pine, cedar, birch, yew, white elm, ash, willow, and "several others unknown to us." He also saw wild peas, gooseberries, strawberries, raspberries, lyme grass, wild wheat, and roses.

WHAT'S THAT IN THE WATER?

☛ **Swimming mammals puzzle observers**

In the St. Lawrence, Cartier reported seeing animals "like horses, which go on land at night but in the daytime remain in the water." They were walruses. The Frenchmen also saw white, or Beluga, whales. Cartier said they had heads and bodies like a greyhound.

My Explorer Journal

★ **Using the picture on this page, write a description or draw an illustration of a walrus for someone who has never seen one.**

Did you know?

The Beluga whale is now endangered in Canada. In the Gulf of St. Lawrence, fewer than 1,000 survive—and possibly as few as 500.

FUR HE'S A JOLLY GOOD FELLOW

★ **Beavers get away with it ... for now**

The native peoples traded with Cartier for animal furs. In the beginning, Cartier was not too interested in trading for furs. However, a century later, fur became so valuable it would become the main reason for the French to set up colonies in Canada.

THAT'S A BIT FISHY

+ **Meat tastes of fish**

On Isle des Oiseaux, Cartier also saw a bird he called *apponats*, or Great Auk, which is now extinct. Cartier's men shot enough to fill two boats in half an hour. They ate some and stored the rest in barrels. The men liked the taste of auk so much that on their second voyage they shot just as many.

Fortune Hunting

Cartier wanted to make a fortune by being the first to find a northwest route to China. When that failed, he looked for other ways to become rich in Canada.

Did you know?

Much of the only known overland route to China was through deserts. Merchants traveled together for safety on groups of camels, called a caravan.

CHINA AHOY

- Explorer seeks route to China
- Wants to cut overland journey

In Cartier's time, Europeans could only trade with Asia by traveling overland. The route was long and slow, and it was controlled by Italians from Venice and by **Muslim** kingdoms. If Cartier could find a western passage to Asia, it would make France—and him—very rich.

A CENTURY TOO EARLY

+ Ahead of the fashion trends

Asia was known for its valuable goods such as spices, silk, and gold. The New World became known for its animal furs. Not very valuable at first, a fashion craze for hats made from beaver fur swept Europe in the next century. Suddenly fur was in demand—and worth a fortune.

ARE WE THERE YET?

★ **Stories of a wealthy kingdom**

★ **Rapids block the way**

Cartier was **motivated** by stories of the riches of the kingdom of Saguenay, which the Iroquois said lay inland. They may have made up the stories to encourage Cartier to move on from Iroquois territory. While in France, Donnacona convinced King Francis I that he could find many valuable goods there. Back in Canada, Cartier traveled up the St. Lawrence to try to find the kingdom in September 1541, but rapids blocked his way. He returned to Charlesbourg Royal. After a hard winter, he went home to France without looking for Saguenay again.

Rapids

The Lachine Rapids on the St. Lawrence River were named using the French word *Chine*, which means China. Explorers believed they blocked their way to China.

STRIKING IT RICH

☛ **Explorers collect "gold"**

☛ **Shows up as fools!**

Cartier and his men thought they had found diamonds and gold. Cartier was so eager to show the treasure to the king it was one reason he rushed home to France. But once home, they found out that the diamonds were ordinary **quartz**. The gold was worthless iron pyrite, now also called "fool's gold."

This Isn't What It Said in the Brochure!

Cartier's time in New France was not always easy. Not only did he face bitterly cold winters and the threat of disease, he also upset his native allies—and his superiors in France.

DOCTOR, DOCTOR!

- Europeans suffer mystery illness
- Chief's son has miracle cure

During the winter of 1535–1536 at Stadacona, Cartier's men suffered from a mysterious illness. They felt weak and had swollen legs and rotting gums. We now know the disease was **scurvy**, which is caused by a lack of Vitamin C. About 25 men died. But Donnacona's son Domagaya showed them how to make a kind of tea from the white spruce or white cedar tree that acted as a natural cure. Soon all of Cartier's men were drinking the herbal tea. In later years, fresh fruits and vegetables were also found to cure scurvy.

Did you know?

Sailors who spent long periods at sea without any fresh food often suffered from scurvy. When the disease was better understood, ships carried citrus fruit such as lemons for sailors.

UNDER ATTACK

★ **Relations turn violent**

★ **Cartier gives up**

On his third return to Canada in 1541, Cartier took two longboats upriver to Hochelaga. The Iroquois there had heard about his settlement at Charlesbourg Royal and did not want to give up that land to the Europeans. When he arrived, the Iroquois attacked Charlesbourg Royal, killing about 35 people. Finally Cartier abandoned the settlement. Roberval tried to stay, but less than two years later he was forced to give up, too.

Attacks

The Iroquois were largely peaceful toward the French. But the Iroquois were also great warriors. They fought often with their enemies, the Algonquian and the Huron.

YOU'LL PAY FOR THIS!

+ **Explorer disobeys orders**

Roberval was commander of Cartier's final expedition. After Cartier abandoned Charlesbourg Royal, Roberval ordered him to return. Instead, Cartier sailed away to France at night. He could have been hanged for disobeying his superior. He managed to survive, but it cost him the king's favor.

My Explorer Journal

★ **Cartier sailed back to France without the permission of Roberval. He may have been punished for this by the king. Imagine you are Cartier and justify your decision to leave. Explain your reasons.**

End of the Road

Cartier sailed home to France in 1542. He had had enough of exploring—and he had not made his fortune. But his travels would later lead to a great age of French settlement in Canada.

HOMETOWN HERO!

☛ **Famous explorer returns**

☛ **Lives quietly at home**

After his return to France, Cartier retired to his birthplace, St. Malo, where he lived quietly in a fine stone house with his wife. In 1545, he published an account of his voyages. He was highly respected and was often called on to be a godfather to children or to settle disputes. He died at the age of 66, on September 1, 1557.

WE GIVE UP!

★ **French abandon North America... for now**

Canada seemed to have no valuable resources. After Roberval gave up settlement, the French abandoned their attempts to explore Canada for decades. A Spanish map drawn of the St. Lawrence River soon after noted that "many Frenchmen died of hunger."

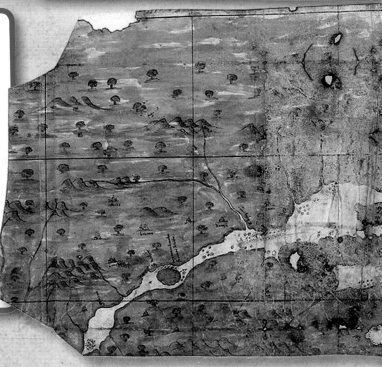

SHOWING THE WAY

- ☞ **Explorer's legacy lasts for centuries**
- ☞ **Opens the way to settlement**

> " Several men and women came to lead us up the mountain, which we had named Mont Royal."
>
> *Jacques Cartier on the future site of Montreal*

Later French settlement of Canada followed the route set by Cartier. Ships sailed up the St. Lawrence to Quebec City and Montreal. Both settlements were based on sites established by Cartier. His exploration laid the way for the future development of Canada. Not only that: he had also given the future country its name.

A NEW ERA

+ **Champlain follows Cartier's footsteps**

+ **New land promising for settlement**

Over 50 years after Cartier's death, the French explorer Samuel de Champlain returned to the St. Lawrence River. He ushered in a new age of French exploration that was shaped by Cartier's achievements in pushing forward into the heart of Canada.

GLOSSARY

astrolabe An instrument used to measure the height of the sun or stars above the horizon

cartographer A person who makes maps

colony A settlement or territory that is under the political control of a different country

compass A device used for navigation with a needle that always points to the north

constellations Recognizable patterns of stars in the sky

cultivated To have grown a plant as a crop for food

cure To preserve an animal skin by using chemicals to dry it

hatchets Small axes for use in one hand

kidnapped To have taken someone captive against his or her will

lateen A large, triangular-shaped sail that helps a ship to sail against the wind

latitude A measure of how far a location is north or south of the Equator

motivated To have given someone a reason to do something

Muslim Follower of the Islamic religion

navigation The ability to find one's way to a particular destination

New World The name given to North, Central, and South America by Europeans after they discovered these lands existed

Northwest Passage A water route to Asia from the Atlantic Ocean through the Canadian Arctic to the Pacific Ocean

palisade A defensive wall made from upright wooden stakes

pilot A sailor who is skilled at navigating in a particular area of water

pole star A name for the North Star, which is often used by sailors for navigation

preserve To treat food by drying or salting it in order to make it last

quartz A hard, crystal-like, translucent mineral that is often colored

resources Useful things that can be gathered from a region, such as minerals from the ground, wood from trees, or fur from animals

scurvy A disease caused by a lack of Vitamin C. Sufferers bleed under their skin and can die.

December 31: Jacques Cartier is born in the port of St. Malo, in Brittany, France.

Around this time, Cartier begins his career as a sailor, probably making voyages to Newfoundland and Brazil.

April: King Francis I asks Cartier to sail west on his first voyage to find a sea route to Asia.

October: Cartier takes Chief Donnacona's two sons and sails home to France.

1491   **1520**   **1524**   **1534**

Cartier marries Mary Catherine des Granches, who comes from one of St. Malo's leading families.

Giovanni da Verrazzano explores the east coast of North America on behalf of the king of France.

July: Cartier lands in what is now Canada and claims the land for France; he meets the local Iroquois.

ON THE WEB

www.historymuseum.ca/ virtual-museum-of-new-france/ the-explorers/jacques-cartier-1534-1542/
Entry on Jacques Cartier from the Canadian Museum of History.

www.history.com/topics/ exploration/jacques-cartier
Biography of Cartier.

www.thecanadianencyclopedia. ca/en/article/jacques-cartier/
Entry on Cartier from Historica Canada, with links to many related articles.

www.softschools.com/timelines/ jacques_cartier_timeline/69/
Timeline of Cartier's life.

BOOKS

Kjelle, Marylou Morano. *Jacques Cartier* (What's So Great About?). Mitchell Lane Publishers, 2006.

Lackey, Jennifer. *Jacques Cartier: Exploring the St. Lawrence River* (In the Footsteps of Explorers). Crabtree Publishing Company, 2011.

Petrie, Kristen. *Jacques Cartier* (Explorers). Checkerboard Library, 2004.

Santella, Andrew. *Jacques Cartier* (Groundbreakers: Explorers). Heinemann Library, 2002.

Woog, Adam. *Jacques Cartier* (Great Explorers). Chelsea House Publishers, 2009.

May: Cartier sails back to Canada on his second voyage and sails up the St. Lawrence River to what is now Montreal, where rapids block his way.

May: Cartier returns to France; this time he kidnaps a number of Iroquois; all but one of them will die in France.

Cartier and his men spend the winter at Charlesbourg Royal, where they come under attack from the Iroquois.

March 19: Disobeying orders from Roberval, Cartier sails home to France.

1535

1536

1541

1542

1557

November: The French prepare to spend the winter in Fort Stadacona; they suffer from scurvy, which they cure with a native remedy.

May: Cartier makes a third voyage to Canada under the command of Jean-François de La Rocque de Roberval; this time he is looking for the land of Saguenay described by the Iroquois.

September 1: Cartier dies after spending his last years quietly, with his wife, in St. Malo.

INDEX